Christianity:
Signs, Symbols, and Stories

Cath Senker

PowerKiDS
press.

New York

Published in 2010 by The Rosen Publishing Group Inc.
29 East 21st Street, New York, NY 10010

Copyright © 2010 Wayland/
The Rosen Publishing Group, Inc.

First Edition

Library of Congress Cataloging-in-Publication Data

Senker, Cath.
  Christianity: signs, symbols, stories / Cath Senker.
      p. cm. -- (Religious signs, symbols, and stories)
  Includes index.
  ISBN 978-1-4358-3037-0 (library binding)
  ISBN 978-1-4358-3045-5 (paperback)
  ISBN 978-1-4358-3053-0 (6-pack)
  1. Christianity--Juvenile literature.
  2. Rites and ceremonies--Juvenile literature.
  3. Christian art and symbolism--Juvenile literature.
  I. Title.
  BR125.5.S46 2010
  246'.55--dc22

                                      2008051910

Manufactured in China

Disclaimer
Although every effort has been made to offer accurate and clearly expressed information, the author and publisher acknowledge that some explanations may not be relevant to those who practice their faith in a different way.

Acknowledgements
The author and publisher would like to thank the following for their pictures to be reproduced in this publication: Cover illustrations: Emmanuel Cerisier (both); ArkReligion.com/Alamy: 10, 14, 22; Bernadette Delaney/Alamy: 23; Chris Fairclough: 6 (both), 12, 15, 16, 19; Con Tanasiuk/ Design Pictures/Corbis: 24; Image Source/Corbis: 4; Jenny Matthews/Alamy: 20; Mike Theiss/Ultimate Chase/Corbis: 5; Oswald Rivas/Reuters/Corbis: 26; Sebastian Pfuetze/zefa/Corbis: 18.

The author would like to thank the following for permission to reproduce material in this book: p.9 Snowman Poem, by Maureen Spell; p.17 Communion bread recipe from Cooks.com; p.21 Story from County Clare Folk-Tales and Myths by Thomas Johnson Westropp, County Clare Library; p.23 Song from Christian Songs for Children, Sowerby Bridge, England (Sheet and instrumental music available from http://patamb.supanet.com/lambs/Communion.html); p.29 Story adapted from The Symbolism of the Ukrainian Easter egg, www.uazone.net/holidays/EasterEggs.html

With special thanks to Sam Dilkes.

The author and publisher would like to thank the following models: Celine Clark, Isobel Grace, Hari Johal, and Charlie Pengelly.

Note to parents and teachers: The projects in this book are designed to be made by children. However, we do recommend adult supervision at all times since the Publisher cannot be held responsible for any injury caused while undertaking any activities.

Contents

Activities

There are lots of activities throughout this book.

You can **read** stories, folk tales, holy stories, and poems on pages 7, 9, 11, 13, 15, 21, 29.

You can **sing** songs on page 23.

You can **make** traditional food on pages 17, 25.

You can **make** crafts and draw pictures on 5, 19, 27.

Signs and symbols

A sign usually has one clear meaning. There are examples of signs on the street. A "stop" sign means just what it says!

A symbol can have many meanings. Think about the different meanings of a cross symbol. A cross can mean you have gotten a sum wrong. It can be a symbol to mark your place in a game such as tic-tac-toe. The cross is also the most common Christian symbol.

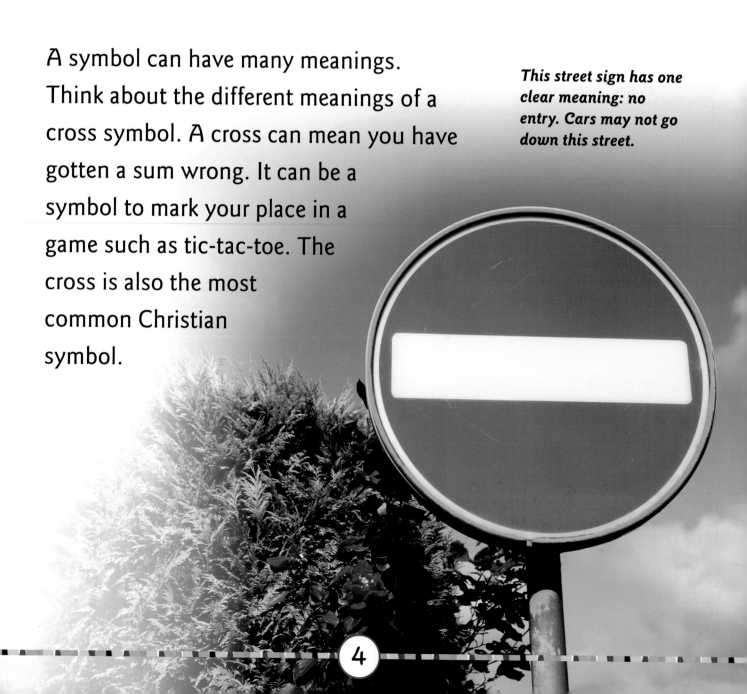

This street sign has one clear meaning: no entry. Cars may not go down this street.

Let's draw a picture

The cross

Think of different ways a cross can be used as a symbol. Draw pictures showing where you might find the symbol. Here are some examples.

The Red Cross

The Red Cross gives medical aid to people in wars. This symbol is on buildings and medical vehicles such as ambulances.

The Christian cross

The Latin Christian cross has a long stem. The Greek Christian cross has four equal arms.

A cross on a ballot paper

When people vote in elections, they sometimes vote for a person by marking the ballot (voting) paper with a cross.

The Christian Cross

Christians follow the teachings of Jesus. Jesus died on a cross. Christians believe that he died to save all of humankind. When Christians see a cross, it reminds them of Jesus.

Some Christians make the sign of the cross to **bless** themselves, other people, or objects. They trace a cross on their body, from the forehead to the chest and from shoulder to shoulder. They make this blessing during prayer or in times of need or danger.

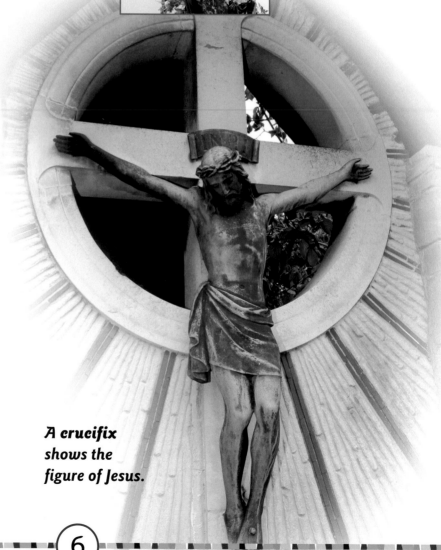

You often see a cross like this inside a church.

A crucifix shows the figure of Jesus.

The Three Trees

Once upon a time, there were three trees on the top of a mountain. The first dreamt of being a treasure chest. The second wanted to be sailing ship. The third wanted to stay on the mountaintop, growing bigger and bigger.

One day, three woodcutters arrived. They chopped down the trees and sent them all away to different workshops. One became a feeding trough, or manger, for animals in a stable. When baby Jesus was born, his mother placed him in that very manger. The second tree became a fishing boat. One stormy night, Jesus used it to shelter from a storm. The third was turned into a wooden beam—and became the cross on which Jesus died. From a simple beam, it became a worldwide symbol of the Christian religion.

The Holy Trinity

Christians believe there is one God who made the world. He is also three: the Father, the Son, and the **Holy Spirit**. Christians call this the **Holy Trinity**.

God is the Father of Jesus, who is the Son. Christians believe that God is a perfect father. He loves and cares for his people, and protects them.

In Ireland, St. Patrick used the clover leaf with three leaves on one stem to explain the Trinity.

The Holy Spirit is God's power working in the world. The Holy Spirit is like the wind. You cannot see it, but you can feel it, and it is powerful.

Trinity poem

When you see a snowman
Three snowballs round,
He is reminding you
That in God, Three in One are found.

The bottom reminds us of God the
    Father,
Our strong rock and foundation
The Creator of all living things,
People, tribes, and nations.

The middle shows us God the Son
With His arms spread open wide.
Who died on the cross for each of us
Our sins, Jesus' blood did hide.

The head reminds us of God the
    Holy Spirit
Who is our counselor [adviser] and
    friend,
He speaks to our hearts and minds
Transforming us in the likeness of
    Him.

So when you see a snowman
In the midst of all the wintertime fun,
Listen carefully and he'll tell you,
"Remember God is Three in One."

By Maureen Spell

The fish

The first Christians lived under Roman rulers. The Romans **persecuted** them because they did not worship Roman gods. Sometimes they rounded up Christians and put them to death.

The fish symbol is still used today. Some Christians have a car bumper sticker with the symbol on it.

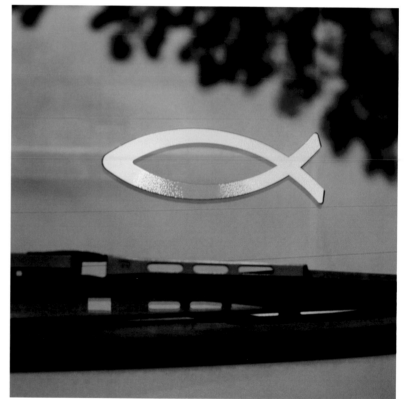

The Christians followed their faith in secret. They used the fish symbol as a secret sign to recognize each other.

Christians also believed there was a secret message in the Greek word for fish, *ixthus*. The six letters are the first letters of the words Jesus, Christ, God, Son, and **Savior** in Greek.

The origin of
the fish symbol

In the days of the early Church, Christians had to hide their faith from the Romans. They needed a secret symbol so they would know if another person was a Christian and could be trusted. The fish was an obvious choice. Many Bible verses mentioned fish, and a fish was quick and simple to draw. To make the secret symbol, one person casually made an arc with their toe on the earth. If the other person was a Christian, he or she drew another arc to complete the fish drawing. Then the two could speak openly without fear.

11

The Bible

The Christian Bible includes the holy books of the Jews and the Christians. It contains many symbols that help people to understand God. For example, mountains stand for strong kingdoms. Hills stand for less powerful kingdoms. Valleys stand for the poor and humble. What might the symbols in this Bible verse mean?

"Every valley shall be filled, and every mountain and hill shall be made low."
(Isaiah 40:4)

It could mean that the kingdoms will be brought down and the ordinary people lifted up, so that all are equal.

A Christian boy reads his children's Bible at bedtime.

Noah's Ark

God created a beautiful world. After a while, though, he saw that people were acting badly. They were fighting, stealing, and telling lies. The only good people were Noah and his family. God decided to destroy everyone on earth, except for Noah's family. He told Noah to build an **ark** *to save his family and a pair of every kind of animal. It was a long and tiring job building the ark and loading on all the animals. At last it was done.*

Soon after, God sent a flood to cover the earth and kill every living thing. Only Noah's family and the animals on the Ark were saved. When the rain finally stopped, Noah sent a dove to find land. It returned with an olive branch, showing that the floods had gone down and the land was dry. The dove was a symbol of the Holy Spirit and of peace—a symbol that God had ended his war with the human race.

Light

Light stops darkness and helps living things. For Christians, it is a symbol of God's presence.

It is also a symbol for Jesus. In church, people light one single candle to remind them of Jesus, who is the light of the world. They place two candles on the **altar** to stand for Jesus' human and godly natures.

A candle is also a symbol of prayer. Roman **Catholics** and **Orthodox Christians** light a candle before an image of Jesus or a saint and say a prayer.

At Easter, people light a candle called the Paschal candle, which stands for Jesus rising again after his death.

Bible verse

In this Bible verse, Jesus explains that being in the light means treating others well.

*"I am the Light of the world.
He who follows Me shall not
walk in darkness,
But have the Light of Life.
He who says he is in the Light,*

*But hates his brother,
Is in darkness until now.
He who loves his brother abides [lives] in the Light,
And there is no cause for stumbling in him.*

*But he who hates his brother is in darkness
And walks in darkness,
And does not know where he is going,
Because the darkness has blinded his eyes."*

(John 8.12; 1 John 2.9–11)

Holy Communion and Eucharist

Eucharist, or **Mass** or **Holy Communion** for Roman Catholics, is the most important act of worship for many Christians. Eucharist means "to give thanks." At the Eucharist, people remember Jesus' **Last Supper** before he died.

This boy is taking Holy Communion in his church.

At the service, the **minister** or **priest** blesses bread and wine. Everyone takes a small piece of bread and a sip of wine. The bread stands for the body of Jesus and the wine stands for his blood. It reminds Christians of what Jesus did for them. It is a way of thanking God for his gifts.

Let's make communion bread

Recipe for communion bread

Ask an adult to help you cook

You will need:

1 cup white flour
1 cup whole-wheat flour
3/4 teaspoon salt
2 tablespoons melted butter
2 tablespoons honey
3/4 cup water

1. Mix the whole-wheat flour and salt in a large bowl and then add the butter, honey, and water.

2. Beat the mixture with a wooden spoon until smooth, then add the white flour a little at a time. Beat it in until the dough is still soft, but dry enough to handle.

3. Knead the dough by folding and punching it for 6 to 8 minutes, until it is smooth and springy.

4. Make into circles roughly 6 inches (15 cm) in diameter and 1/2 inch (1 cm) thick.

5. Place the circles on a greased baking sheet. With a sharp knife, cut a crisscross grid of lines 1/2 inch (1 cm) apart. Make sure the cuts are deep and go all the way to the edge.

6. Bake at 375° F (190° C) for 25 minutes or until the top is light golden brown.

7. Cool on a wire rack before eating.

Meanings of colors

For Christians, colors have meanings. The cloths on the altar, **lectern**, and **pulpit** and the priest's or minister's robes change according to the **cycles** of the Christian year. There is a Christmas cycle and an Easter cycle. Within each cycle, these colors are used for the different times of the year:

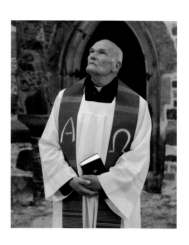

Priests sometimes wear purple robes.

Purple: in the seasons preparing for a festival—**Advent** and **Lent**. Purple stands for fasting and asking forgiveness for doing wrong.

White: festivals of Easter, **Ascension Day**, and Christmas. White stands for purity, light, and celebration.

Red: **Holy Week** and **Pentecost** (Whitsun). Red stands for the Holy Spirit. At Pentecost, Christians remember how Jesus' first followers became filled with the Holy Spirit. They gained the power to spread Jesus' teachings. Red is used during Holy Week to stand for the blood of Christ. A priest or minister might also wear red robes.

Green: other times. It stands for growth in the Christian faith.

Pie chart of the church year

You will need:

Paper
A compass to draw a circle
Ruler
Colored pencils

1. Draw a circle on your paper.

2. Copy this pie chart below showing the church year.

3. Color in the segments with the colors the church uses at that time of year.

Advent

Christmas

Epiphany

Ash Wednesday
Lent

Holy Week

Easter Day
Easter
Ascension

Pentecost

Rest of the church year

Baptism

Most Christians **baptize** babies with water. Baptism marks the start of a new life with God. During baptism, the priest or minister sprinkles water on the baby's head. Water is a symbol that the baby is pure and clean. Because water is refreshing, it is also a symbol that baptism brings happiness to the baby.

At the baptism, the baby wears white, which stands for purity

A candle is lit to **symbolize** Jesus, who brought light to the world. The priest makes the sign of the cross on the baby's forehead to show he or she belongs to Christ. The parents and **godparents** promise that the baby will live life as a good Christian.

The baptism of Senán

In Moylough, County Clare, in Ireland, a woman gave birth to a baby. One morning, when he was still tiny and not yet baptized, she was walking along with him. The woman was hungry and hadn't had time to prepare a meal. She stopped and ate some wild fruit to keep her going. "You have an early appetite, mother," said the tiny baby. "You have old talk, my child," she replied. She decided to name him Senán, from sean, meaning "old."

The mother now wanted to baptize her baby. Strangely for Ireland, which is a rainy country, there was no water at hand. Senán told his mother to pull up three rushes, and to her amazement, a lake appeared. Senán was baptized in the lake, which today is called Loughshanan. He grew up to become a great saint.

First Holy Communion and Confirmation

When children are old enough to understand what it means to be a Christian, they have their **confirmation**, or **First Holy Communion** then confirmation if they are Catholics. At the confirmation ceremony, the **bishop** asks them questions about their beliefs, and they promise to live a good Christian life. The bishop places his hand on each child's head. It is a symbol of the strength that the Holy Spirit will bring the child.

In the Catholic Church, the bishop draws the sign of the cross in oil on the child's forehead. It is a sign of being chosen by God.

At the confirmation ceremony, the child wears white as a symbol of purity.

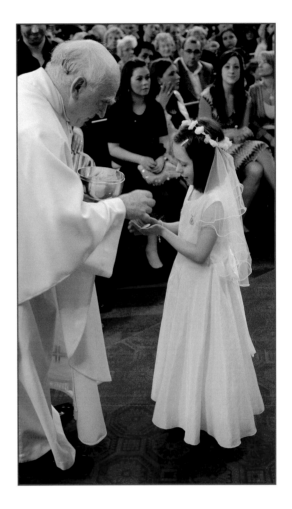

First Holy Communion Song

The waiting is over and this is the day
The nerves and the worries have all gone away
I'm ready to meet you in this special way
Come meet me, Lord Jesus, meet me
The bread and wine you offer free
Are symbols of your love for me
Come, sweet Jesus, meet me.

My teachers, my family, my friends, and my priest
Have helped me prepare for the forthcoming feast
For all other things, I don't care in the least
Come meet me, Lord Jesus, meet me
Each and every day's been spent
Preparing for this sacrament [important religious ceremony]
Come, sweet Jesus, meet me.

Preparing for Easter

During Lent, people prepare for Easter. Lent lasts for 40 days (not including Sundays) and ends on the day before Easter Sunday.

The day before Lent starts is **Shrove Tuesday**, a day of celebration. In the past, people did not eat meat, fish, fat, eggs, or dairy foods during Lent. They made pancakes to use up all the food that could not be eaten in Lent. Pancake Day is the symbol of this custom.

Christians go to church during Lent to ask for forgiveness for their sins.

Lent is a serious time. Christians remember how Jesus spent 40 days in the desert fasting and praying, while the devil tried to tempt him. They ask God to forgive them for things they have done wrong. Some people **fast** or give up their favorite foods to symbolize Jesus' suffering.

Let's make pancakes

Recipe for pancake day

You will need:

1 cup (115 g) self-rising flour
1/4 teaspoon baking soda
1/4 teaspoon salt
1 large egg
1 tablespoon sugar
1 cup (275 ml) milk
2 tablespoons oil

1. Sift the flour, soda, salt, and sugar into a mixing bowl and make a well in the middle.

2. Break the egg into the well. Beat the egg so that it starts to mix with the flour from around the bowl.

3. Add the milk a little at a time. Add the oil. Mix everything together until the batter is smooth and thick.

4. Heat a little butter in a frying pan.

5. Pour about 2 tablespoons of the batter into the pan. Cook on medium heat for about 60 seconds until the pancake starts to form bubbles. Flip it and cook the other side.

6. Keep the pancake warm and repeat with the rest of the batter to make a stack.

Ask an adult to help you cook

Palm Sunday

Holy Week is the week leading up to Easter Sunday. It is the most serious week of the Christian year.

Palm Sunday is the first day of Holy Week. Christians remember how Jesus entered Jerusalem on a donkey for the **Passover** feast. The crowds cheered him and laid palm leaves on the ground. This was how a king was welcomed in those days.

A child waves palm crosses on the Palm Sunday procession.

In memory of the story, worshipers carry palm leaves or homemade palm crosses. They go on a procession in and around the church.

Let's make a palm cross

Palm cross

You will need:

Sheet of card
Ruler
Pencil
Scissors
Stapler

1. Cut two strips of card 2/3 in. (1.5 cm) wide.

2. Make the crossbeam. On one strip, mark from the left 3/4 in. (2 cm), 1 1/2 in. (4 cm), 4 in. (10 cm), and 8 in. (20 cm).

3. Fold from the right along the 8 in. (20 cm) and then the 4 in. (10 cm) line.

4. Turn the card over. Fold forward along the 3/4 in. (2 cm) and then the 1 1/2 in. (4 cm) line. This makes the center of the crossbeam. Flatten the card.

5. Make the cross. Insert one end of the other strip of card under the top layer of the center of the crossbeam.

6. Fold the long piece of card behind the crossbeam. Thread it up in front of it and then under the top layer of the center of the crossbeam. Pull it through and flatten it.

7. Thread the long piece of card back under the center of the crossbeam. Stop when a cross shape is made.

8. Secure your cross with a staple in the center. Ask an adult to help you with the stapler. If you need help with this activity, please see the websites on page 31.

Easter

On the Friday after Palm Sunday, the Roman rulers arrested Jesus and put him to death on the cross. Christians call this day Good Friday, because Jesus showed his goodness by dying for the sake of humankind.

You can dip hard-boiled eggs in half a cup of water, 1 tablespoon of vinegar, and food coloring. Let the eggs dry and you will have colorful eggs for Easter!

The Bible says that on the Sunday, Jesus rose from the dead. His followers were amazed to see him alive again.

On Easter Sunday, people remember this extraordinary event. They decorate Easter eggs and give Easter baskets full of candy eggs. Eggs are a symbol of new life. Christians believe that death is not the end. Jesus is still alive, with God in heaven. When people die, they, too, start a new life with God.

A Ukrainian folk tale

When Jesus was dying on the cross, blood flowing from his wounds fell on the ground. Wherever a drop fell, a red egg was created. Jesus' mother, Mary, was standing beneath his cross praying and crying. She gathered all the eggs into a handkerchief. Her tears turned the eggs into elaborate decorated Easter eggs.

Mary went to the ruler, Pontius Pilate, to ask if she could bury her son. On her way there, she gave an Easter egg to all the children she met, telling them to live in peace. When she arrived at the palace, she fainted and dropped the eggs. The Easter eggs rolled all over the world. Since then, people everywhere have decorated eggs at Easter as a symbol of love and peace.

Advent The period of four weeks before Christmas when people prepare for the festival. *Advent* means "coming."

altar The holy table at the front of the church.

ark A huge boat that Noah built to save his family and animals from the flood.

Ascension Day The Thursday 40 days after Easter Sunday when Christians remember Jesus' ascension—when He rose up to heaven.

baptize To welcome a person into the church through a ceremony that involves water.

bishop The religious leader in charge of the churches in a large area called a diocese.

bless To ask God to protect someone or something.

Catholics People who are members of the part of the church that has the Pope as leader.

confirmation A ceremony in which people promise to be good Christians. It is called a confirmation, because they confirm the promises that were made for them when they were baptized.

crucifix A model of a cross with a figure of Jesus Christ on it, as a symbol of the Christian religion.

cycle An order of events that are repeated again and again.

Eucharist A ceremony in which people eat bread and drink wine in memory of the last meal Jesus ate with his followers.

fast To go without food for religious reasons.

First Holy Communion A Roman Catholic ceremony. It is the first time that a young person takes Holy Communion, usually when he or she is about seven or eight years old.

godparents People close to the child's family who promise at the baptism to teach the child about the Christian religion as he or she grows up.

Holy Communion The Roman Catholic form of the Eucharist ceremony, when people eat bread and drink wine in memory of the last meal Jesus ate with his followers.

Holy Spirit The power of God in the world. It helps people to do what God wants.

Holy Trinity The unity of God (the Father), Jesus (the Son), and the Holy Spirit, which together are one God.

Holy Week The week before Easter Sunday.

Last Supper The last meal that Jesus shared with his followers before his arrest and death.

lectern The stand that holds the Bible or notes for the minister's sermon.

Lent The season of 40 days before Easter (not including Sundays). Some Christians give up favorite foods or things they enjoy to remember Jesus' suffering.

Mass A Roman Catholic ceremony to remember the last meal Christ had with his followers.

minister A trained religious leader.

Orthodox Christians Churches such as the Russian and Greek Church. They are sometimes called the Eastern Churches.

Passover A Jewish holiday when people remember how the Jews were freed from slavery in Egypt.

Pentecost (also called Whitsun) A festival 50 days after Easter Sunday. People remember the coming of the Holy Spirit, which helped Jesus' followers spread his teachings.

persecuted When people are treated cruelly and unfairly because of their race, religion, or political beliefs. The early Christians were persecuted because of their religion.

priest A trained religious leader in the Catholic and Episcopalian (Anglican) churches.

pulpit A stand where the minister or priest stands to give the sermon.

Savior A name for Jesus. It means someone who saves people from danger.

Shrove Tuesday The day before the beginning of Lent. It is traditional to eat pancakes to use up eggs and fat, which cannot be eaten during Lent.

symbolize To be a symbol for.

Books to read

Easter (Rookie Read-About Holidays)
by David F Marx (Children's Press, 2001)

*Inside a Catholic Church: A Guide
to Signs, Symbols, and Saints*
by Joseph M Champlin (Orbis Books, 2003)

My Bible Story Book
by Carine Mackenzie (CF4K, 2006)

*Rings, Kings and Butterflies: Lessons
on Christian Symbols for Children*
by Harriet Vandermeer (Augsburg Fortress
Publications, 2006)

Religious Articles: Objects used in Worship
by Anita Ganeri (Steck-Vaughn, 2000)

What You Will See Inside A Catholic Church
by Michael Keane (Skylight Paths Publishing, 2002)

Web Sites

Due to the changing nature of
Internet links, PowerKids Press has
developed an online list of Web sites
related to the subject of this book.
This site is updated regularly. Please
use this link to access this list:
www.powerkidslinks.com/sss/christian

✝ Index